# A Study Guide

FOR

## Exchanging Mirrors

A CALL TO EMBRACE YOUR
GOSPEL-GIVEN IDENTITY

KATHERINE HAGER

# *A Study Guide* for Exchanging Mirrors

Copyright © 2022 Katherine Hager | www.equippedmama.com

All rights reserved. No part of this publication may be reproduced or transmitted for commercial purposes, except for brief quotations in printed reviews, without written permission of the publisher.

ISBN: 978-1-7341581-8-2 (Study Guide)
ISBN: 978-1-7341581-3-7 (Print Book)
ISBN: 978-1-7341581-4-4 (eBook)

Unless otherwise noted, all scripture quotations are taken from the NET Bible® copyright ©1996–2017 by Biblical Studies Press, LLC. netbible.com All rights reserved.

Scripture quotations marked (ESV) are taken from The Holy Bible, English Standard Version. ESV® Text Edition: 2016. Copyright © 2001 by Crossway Bibles, a publishing ministry of Good News Publishers.

Scripture quotations marked (KJV) are taken from the Holy Bible, King James Version (Public Domain).

Scripture quotations marked (NASB) are from the New American Standard Bible 1995, Copyright © 1960, 1971, 1977, 1995 by The Lockman Foundation. All rights reserved.

Scripture quotations marked (NIV) are from the Holy Bible, New International Version®, NIV® Copyright ©1973, 1978, 1984, 2011 by Biblica, Inc.® All rights reserved worldwide.

Scripture quotations marked (NKJV) are from the Holy Bible, New King James Version®. Copyright © 1982 by Thomas Nelson. All rights reserved.

Scripture quotations marked (NLT) are from the Holy Bible, New Living Translation, copyright © 1996, 2004, 2015 by Tyndale House Foundation. All rights reserved.

Book and cover design: Becky's Graphic Design®, LLC
www.beckysgraphicdesign.com

Cover photo by Christina Hastings, www.christinahastings.com

Printed in the United States of America

# Introduction

*"From Peter, an apostle of Jesus Christ"*

1 PETER 1:1A

> *We are constantly encouraged to build a better version of ourselves, to motivate ourselves toward greatness, beauty, and success. For these goals we are also given mirrors. These mirrors tell us if we are living up to our earthly potential and promise to "motivate" us when we fail by using tactics like guilt and shame... (Exchanging Mirrors, pg. 2).*

In what ways do you resonate with these opening thoughts about Peter, the Gospel, and your personal identity? Prayerfully contemplate where you believe the Lord might be asking you to reevaluate your personal ideals or values as you work your way through this study of 1 Peter.

**READ:** 1 Peter 1, *Exchanging Mirrors* pgs. 1-10. Briefly share your personal introduction. Contrast how you introduce yourself to the introduction given at the beginning of 1 Peter.

1. Explore the greetings used in other epistles. What repeated words do the apostles use to describe themselves? (1 Corinthians 1:1, 2 Corinthians 1:1, Ephesians 1:1, Philippians 1:1, James 1:1, 2 Peter 1:1) What insight do these words give you into the lives and testimonies of these men?

2. In Peter's restoration, Jesus asks Peter to confirm his love for Him. He never revisits the painful details of Peter's failure. Peter is given a completely clean slate. Read Romans 8:1-2. Gratitude should be central to a true understanding of our Gospel-given identity. Consider what your identity is *not* because of the Gospel. Are you habitually grateful for this truth?

3. Do you personally understand the Gospel? Is there any part of the Gospel you feel as though you are not able to accept? God's Word is very clear on Salvation, revisit these passages for a fresh understanding of God's plan for forgiveness of sins. (Read Romans 3:23, Romans 6:23, Romans 5:8, 1 Corinthians 15:3-4, 1 John 1:9).

4. Do you reflect the Gospel through your life? Where are areas of your life where you see the Gospel growing you in sanctification, worship, and hope? See James 1:23-24b, 1 Corinthians 13:12 for examples.

5. Revisit the final questions in the introduction:

> *Do you find yourself being changed into Jesus's image, worshipping His attributes, and longing for His presence? Or do you find yourself looking at Jesus on a self-seeking manner, as a means to an improved version of yourself? (pg. 10).*

As you begin this study, take some time to consider these questions. Are you seeking the Lord out of ulterior motives? Perhaps for your own upward mobility? To conquer a fear or an addiction? Confess any wrong motivations and ask the Lord to give you a heart that desires a deeper love for *Him*, rather than simply what He has to offer.

# Notes

_____

_____

_____

_____

_____

# Prayer Requests

_____

_____

_____

_____

_____

_____

## CHAPTER ONE
## Chosen

*"...who are chosen according to the foreknowledge of God the Father by being set apart by the Spirit for obedience and for sprinkling with Jesus Christ's blood. May grace and peace be yours in full measure!"*

(1 PETER 1:1B-2)

*You are set apart. Much like a valuable necklace is stored with care and used for special occasions, those who are chosen are also set apart to display God's love and forgiveness. We are removed from our sinful lives and earthly passions for salvation and to showcase God's kindness. (Exchanging Mirrors, pg. 13).*

If you are a Christ-follower, do you understand with your heart and your head the truth that you have been chosen by God for salvation? This truth should radically impact the day-to-day "operations" of your life. As you read this chapter and complete the study questions, consider how this truth ought to impact your everyday life.

**READ:** 1 Peter- highlight the words "grace" and "peace" throughout the text. Note the instances in which these words are used throughout the epistle. *Exchanging Mirrors* pgs. 11-25.

1. In what ways do you see culture articulate that grace and peace are circumstantial? How can Christ-followers live the truth through our actions and words?

2. Define grace and peace, using a dictionary if necessary. In what ways have we been shown grace? For what reasons ought we to have peace?

3. What attributes of God are revealed through Peter's use of the word "foreknowledge"? Read also Acts 2:23. How do these attributes of God impact your understanding of the Gospel?

4. Read Paul's warning against false teachers in 2 Timothy 3:2-7. How does this warning cause you to view doctrinal error?

5. In Chapter One the author states of Empowerment that:

> *This philosophy is flawed because egocentrism, rather than God's glory, is the driving force...It shifts our focus from fulfilling our life's purpose of honoring God to self-gratification. The gospel becomes us-centered and us-sized. Rather than praising the Lord for saving us from our hopeless depravity, we flatter ourselves that Jesus chose us because we would make good Christians. (Exchanging Mirrors, pg. 19.)*

Read 1 Timothy 1:15-17. Consider Paul's testimony compared to the author's perspective on the "empowered" gospel. How do these gospels differ?

6. Read 2 Corinthians 3:18, Galatians 2:20. In what way does the Gospel promise us a better life? In what ways must we reject the desire to be empowered?

# Notes

_____

_____

_____

_____

_____

# Prayer Requests

_____

_____

_____

_____

_____

_____

## CHAPTER 2
# You're Not There Yet

*"From Peter, an apostle of Jesus Christ, to those temporarily residing abroad (in Pontus, Galatia, Cappadocia, the province of Asia, and Bithynia) who are chosen according to the foreknowledge of God the Father by being set apart by the Spirit for obedience and for sprinkling with Jesus Christ's blood. May grace and peace be yours in full measure!"*

1 PETER 1:1-2

*"Suffering is acute and chronic. Suffering is the straight razor that cuts through the fluff of life. In the searing pain of loss, suffering screams that this world is not our home." (Exchanging Mirrors, pg. 30).*

In this chapter, the author explores the unique tutelage of suffering and how a Christ-follower can patiently, even joyfully, walk through suffering because of the hope of the Gospel.

**READ:** 1 Peter, looking to identify warnings of trails, or comfort in trials or suffering. *Exchanging Mirrors* pgs. 27-43.

1. Define suffering in your own words. Do you agree with Elisabeth Elliot's definition of the term on pg. 29?

2. Consider Peter's choice in calling God the "faithful creator" (1 Peter 4:19). Read Revelation 21:1-4. How does knowing that God is the Faithful Creator give you hope in the face of suffering? What specific aspects of hope can all believers look forward to, according to this passage?

3. What are some reasons for hope listed in Peter's prayer of thanksgiving, listed in 1 Peter 1:3-4? Of these, which is the most impactful to you?

4. Why does Peter exhort believers to suffer in a godly manner? (Read 1 Peter 2:12, 2:20, 3:16). What other reasons can you think of for the importance of godly suffering?

5. On pg. 41 the author writes;

   > *Only through the sanctified eyes of suffering can we see our trials from God's perspective. Perhaps we will never understand the reason for our earthly hurts, or perhaps God will give us the grace to echo Joseph's words to those who misuse us: "As for you, you meant to harm me, but God intended it for a good purpose" (Gen. 50:20 a). This is the response of a sanctified saint, one that has responded to suffering and emerged with the proven nature of their faith as gold. (Exchanging Mirrors, pg. 41).*

   Respond to the author's words. Have you ever experienced such a perspective in the face of suffering? Has the Lord ever allowed you to understand the reason behind a trial you faced?

6. How does the concept of not being home yet offer hope and encouragement to those facing trials?

## Notes

_____
_____
_____
_____
_____

## Prayer Requests

_____
_____
_____
_____
_____

## CHAPTER THREE
# Girl Empowered (For Submission)

*"In the same way, wives, be subject to your own husbands. Then, even if some are disobedient to the word, they will be won over without a word by the way you live, when they see your pure and reverent conduct."*

1 PETER 3:1-2

> *"In the same way, wives, be subject to your own husbands." If there was a single sentence that could motivate a woman to put down a book, this is it. Submission leaves an acrid taste in the mouths of many. Women recoil from the idea, either from bad experiences or bad attitudes, because no one naturally desires to submit... (Exchanging Mirrors, pg. 46).*

**READ:** 1 Peter 2:21-25, 3:1-12, Ephesians 5:22-33. *Exchanging Mirrors* pgs. 45-59

1. What is your initial response to Peter's exhortation to submission? Do you struggle with this concept of wives submitting to their husbands? Why or why not?

2. The author highlights how submission points us to the Gospel. Re-read 1 Peter 2:21-25, Mark 14:36. How did Christ serve as the ultimate example of submission?

3. How was Christ glorified after his submission to the Father? (See Philippians 2:8-10). What are benefits of wives submitting to their husbands?

4. In what ways are husbands accountable for the way in which they lead their wives? How does knowledge of this truth encourage wives to submit to their husbands?

5. How does a proper understanding of the Gospel encourage wives to live out this command, even if it requires some sacrifice? (See also Philippians 3:7-8).

6. In what ways is submission a position of power? Have you seen examples of this in your own life?

# Notes

_____

_____

_____

_____

_____

# Prayer Requests

_____

_____

_____

_____

_____

_____

# CHAPTER 4
## But Literally Stop Looking in the Mirror

*"Let your beauty not be external—the braiding of hair and wearing of gold jewelry and fine clothes-- but the inner person of the heart, the lasting beauty of a gentle and tranquil spirit, which is precious in God's sight."*

1 PETER 3:3-4

*Our appearance is not meant to be primarily external. Christian women are to have a beauty that comes from a spirit changed and shaped by the Lord. However, a focus on internal beauty seems almost impossible given the pervasiveness of the mirror-obsessed culture in which we live. (Exchanging Mirrors, pg. 63).*

In this chapter, the author explores the perils of preoccupation with personal appearance. How ought a Christian woman to make herself beautiful? Peter offers some helpful commentary that is sure to always be in style, and flattering for women of all ages.

**READ:** 1 Peter 3, *Exchanging Mirrors* pgs. 61-78.

1. What does the author highlight as a key word when considering appearance as outlined in 1 Peter 3? (Re-read pg. 63) How does this word lend insight into your understanding of godly physical presentation?

2. Reflect on these words from Chapter 4:

> *"The lust fueled by vanity is not fitting for believers; therefore, we must continually work to shift our focus. We must turn from our own reflection to a better one, one that is not passing away and which does last forever."* (Exchanging Mirrors, pgs. 66-67).

How does the Gospel encourage women not to be preoccupied with their physical appearance and offer help to overcome vanity?

3. What lessons can we learn from the life of Esther in regards to physical attire and adornment?

4. What hope does Paul outline for believers concerning the temporary nature of all things- including our bodies? (Read 2 Corinthians 4:16-18, Romans 8:20-23).

5. What adjectives does Paul use in 1 Timothy 2:9-10 for women's attire? (Try reading multiple versions for a more complete understanding). How would you define modest dress?

6. How often do you take time to look at Jesus, and to fix your eyes on His beauty? How can you shift your thoughts from your physical appearance to loving Him and delighting in Him more? Take time this week to talk to the Lord about these things.

# Notes

_____

_____

_____

_____

_____

# Prayer Requests

_____

_____

_____

_____

_____

## CHAPTER 5
# Put Your Game Face On

*"Therefore, get your minds ready for action by being fully sober, and set your hope completely on the grace that will be brought to you when Jesus Christ is revealed."*

1 PETER 1:13

*"Be sober and alert. Your enemy the devil, like a roaring lion, is on the prowl looking for someone to devour."*

1 PETER 5:8

*This is a battle, but we are strengthened and equipped for it by the power of God. Our passivity works against us, our flesh aches for sin, our enemy attacks us openly...In Christ we have the perfect example for victory. (Exchanging Mirrors, pg. 96).*

How ought a Christian to live with sanctified thoughts? Does holiness in thought seem like too difficult a task when the world is filled with endless opportunities to think about sin? Peter offers timely reminders for the Christ-follower to live with a mind trained for right thinking.

**READ:** 1 Peter, looking for specific commands Peter gives to have sober or right thinking, especially in the face of persecution. *Exchanging Mirrors* pgs. 79-96.

1. What areas of your life might be training ground for having a mind obedient to Christ? (See page 81).

2. The author highlights one of the barriers to a disciplined and sober mind as being passivity. She writes:

    *Passivity is fueled by busyness, noise, music, television, even doing "spiritual things." These seemingly good things, when done apart from the Lord's direction and leading, can cause us to wander into apathy. Through the noise this busyness creates, we are robbed of the opportunity to rest at the Lord's feet and to be saturated in His Word. Without constant and intentional abiding with Christ, we risk passivity. (Exchanging Mirrors, pg. 83).*

    Do you agree with the author's assessment of passivity dulling our spiritual awareness? In what ways can you de-clutter your life to allow for increased spiritual growth?

3. In what way does the admonition in Ecclesiastes 12:13-14 encourage or motivate you to a holy thought life?

4. Do you think about the reality of Satan as your enemy? Take time to visit the verses in this chapter outlining his nature. (Read 1 Peter 5:8, Job 1:6-2:8, Jude 1:9). How do these verses exhort or motivate you to a holy thought life?

5. Take some time to read the verses surrounding Jesus's prayer listed in Luke 22:42. How does Jesus's example encourage you as you wrestle with your thought life?

6. Only through God's power can we live a life of victory in our thought lives. Have you thanked the Lord recently for the power He grants to allow us to live lives that please Him? If you are struggling with a particular area of failure in your thought life, consider reading 2 Corinthians 10:3-5 daily, asking the Lord to grant you His power and His strength to live in freedom from sin.

## Notes

_____
_____
_____
_____
_____

## Prayer Requests

_____
_____
_____
_____
_____

# CHAPTER 6
## Keep Talking

*"So get rid of all evil and all deceit and hypocrisy and envy and all slander. And yearn like newborn infants for pure, spiritual milk, so that by it you may grow up to salvation, if you have experienced the Lord's kindness."*

1 PETER 2:1-3

*"For the one who wants to love life and see good days must keep his tongue from evil and his lips from uttering deceit."*

1 PETER 3:10

*Words might cause collateral damage if unchecked, but the true victim of careless speech is the speaker. In doing evil, we turn the Lord's face away from us. No matter the reason for our language, our responses must be pure. Regardless of our circumstances, our conversation must be reverent. (Exchanging Mirrors, pg. 99).*

Compared to some sins, sins of the mouth often are seen as socially acceptable, yet Peter warns against these. As you explore this chapter, consider Peter's warning against deceit, hypocrisy and slander. Why are these three sins so dangerous?

**READ:** 1 Peter, looking for instances of holy speech as outlined in the epistle. *Exchanging Mirrors* pgs. 97-113.

1. What are some of the directions Peter gives for believers' speech? Why might these directions have been especially difficult given the circumstances of the *original* recipients?

2. In your own words, define the three major sins of the mouth discussed in this chapter.

    Deceit—

    Hypocrisy—

    Slander—

3. Meditate on Colossians 3:15-17. How does fellowship as outlined in this passage differ from normal church get-togethers? How can you encourage other believers to have fellowship more like this example?

4. How often are we all guilty of the sin of hypocrisy, treating those within our home (or those with whom we are most comfortable) significantly worse than people elsewhere? Of this sin, the author writes:

> *Hypocrisy is devastating. It communicates through the megaphone of raised voices and sighs of frustration that the family is not deserving of life-giving speech. This articulates a lack of value for the family unit and breeds resentment and hostility between children and parents. (Exchanging Mirrors, pg. 104).*

Are there people in your life who you have hurt with this sin? Have you sought their forgiveness?

5. Why is the eradication of sinful speech so important for a Christ-follower?

6. Does preparation for a platform differ from preparation for the orchestra pit? What does it mean to prepare for either of these positions?

## Notes

_____
_____
_____
_____
_____

## Prayer Requests

_____
_____
_____
_____
_____

# CHAPTER 7
## A Gentle and Quiet Spirit

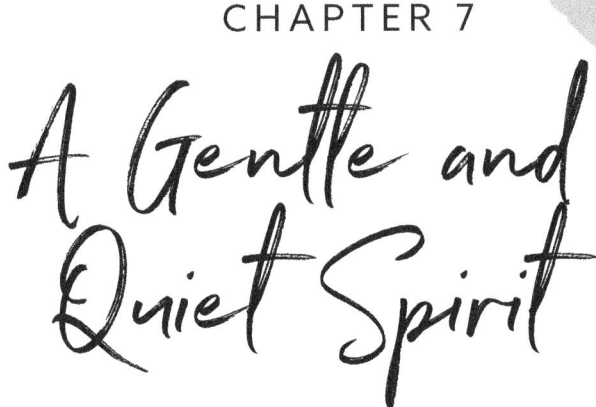

*"Let your beauty not be external... but the inner person of the heart, the lasting beauty of a gentle and tranquil spirit, which is precious in God's sight."*

1 PETER 3:3A, 4

> *Living out the gentleness that is characteristic of the fruit of the Spirit is, humanly speaking, impossible. Praise the Lord we serve the God of the impossible. (Exchanging Mirrors, pg. 119).*

Gentleness and quietness. Two characteristics all too often missing in a culture preoccupied with noise and progress. Yet in displaying these virtues, individuals focused on Jesus are able to minister in a way the world desperately needs and seldom sees.

**READ:** 1 Peter 3, Philippians 4:4-7, Colossians 3:12-13. *Exchanging Mirrors* pgs. 115-132.

1. In what ways does our culture reject the notion of gentleness today?

2. Why must we daily crucify the flesh (Galatians 2:20) and live in the power of the Spirit to be able to live a life of gentleness? (Read also Galatians 5:22-23).

3. In what ways does a rejection of quietness harm our spiritual well-being?

4. Take time to consider how Christ demonstrated a life of quietness and gentleness. How does His example encourage you to more fully embrace these attributes? Read Matthew 9:36, Luke 23:9, Luke 23:42-43, John 11:33-36, John 19:11, and John 19:26-27.

5. Read Daniel 4:34-35. How does developing a trust in the sovereignty of God encourage us to grow in quietness?

6. In what ways can quietness itself serve as a ministry? Do you have any examples of where someone ministered to you in this way?

7. Meditate on the final Scripture passage at the end of the chapter. In what ways does this passage encourage you to grow in either gentleness or quietness?

> *"Stop your striving and recognize that I am God.*
> *I will be exalted over the nations!*
> *I will be exalted over the earth!"*
> *The Lord of Heaven's Armies is on our side!*
> *The God of Jacob is our stronghold! (Selah)*
>
> (PSALM 46:10B-11)

# Notes

## Prayer Requests

## CHAPTER 8

# Love, For Real

*"You have purified your souls by obeying the truth in order to show sincere mutual love. So love one another earnestly from a pure heart. You have been born anew, not from perishable but from imperishable seed, through the living and enduring word of God."*

1 PETER 1:22-23

*Jesus is the picture of love. Jesus is love perfected. Jesus is our model, mentor, and the method by which we are able to love. (Exchanging Mirrors, pg. 139).*

Christlike love radically differs from the cultural perception of love. Through living out *this* love, followers in the Lord Jesus can model the Gospel to a world that desperately needs to understand what true love is.

**READ:** 1 Peter 1:13-25, John 15:12-17, 1 Corinthians 13, *Exchanging Mirrors* pgs. 133-148.

1. How does our culture define love? Using some of the Scriptures provided above, how does the Bible define love?

2. In what ways does an inaccurate understanding of love hinder us from truly loving others?

3. How can Christ-followers mirror the Gospel in our love for one another? Read 1 Peter 1:22-23.

4. On pages 138-139 the author highlights verses of how Jesus Christ modeled 1 Corinthians 13 love for others during His time on earth. Take time to look up some of the verses provided in this chapter. How does Christ's consistent demonstration of this agape love encourage you to love Him more or serve Him better?

5. How does a right understanding of the nature of God shape the command to love "earnestly from a pure heart?" (1 Peter 1:22b)

6. In what ways did Christ teach and model a counter-cultural understanding of love? Read Luke 6:27-29, 31, John 13:1-5.

7. In what ways might the Lord be calling you to live out this sincere, mutual love in your life?

## Notes

_____

_____

_____

_____

_____

## Prayer Requests

_____

_____

_____

_____

_____

# CHAPTER 9
# With All Your Authority

*"Give a shepherd's care to God's flock among you, exercising oversight not merely as a duty but willingly under God's direction, nor for shameful profit but eagerly. And do not lord it over those entrusted to you, but be examples to the flock."*

1 PETER 5:2-3

> *Endeavors may dissolve, children might rebel, and homes may slip into disarray, but regardless of the outcome, Christ sees our labors. The One who knows our hearts and sees our service in secret is the One who will give us our eternal reward for the work we have done. (Exchanging Mirrors, pg. 166).*

Care for your flock. Peter exhorts church leaders to care for the needs of those within their oversight, however, women can glean much wisdom from these practical instructions. We have all been delegated authority to use within our spheres of influence, and we are wise to know how to use it well.

**READ:** 1 Peter 5, Proverbs 31:25-31. *Exchanging Mirrors* pgs. 149-166.

1. Identify individuals who are your authority. Who are you in authority over? You may wish to add to this list as you read through Chapter 9.

2. How does the centurion's story in Matthew 8 demonstrate a proper understanding of authority? In what way did this man amaze Jesus?

3. Read some of the passages provided in this chapter of Biblically-commended female authority (see Judges 4:4-7, Esther 4:14, 7:3-4. Luke 1:42-45, Romans 16:1-2, 2 Timothy 1:5). How do these women's examples help you understand the Biblical concept of female authority?

4. In what ways might the Lord be calling you to care for the flock that He has given you? Are there physical or spiritual needs that you should be filling for those within your sphere of influence?

5. Which of the three wrong authority mentalities is the biggest struggle for you (See pgs. 160-163)? How does leading grudgingly, for personal profit, or to hold the position over others hinder us from Christ-centered leadership?

6. Of Gospel-centered authority, the author writes:

> *The benefits of gospel-focused authority are reflected in immediate improvements and long-term rewards. The immediate improvements are found in pursuing your position of authority to the best of your ability, full-throttle, and fully submitted to God's will, under authority and in authority... Far surpassing the value of an orderly home, well-run business, or pleasantly behaved children, the ultimate reward of faithful shepherding is granted by Christ Himself." (Exchanging Mirrors, pgs. 165-166).*

How does this understanding of authority encourage you to lead those the Lord has placed in your care?

## Notes

_____
_____
_____
_____
_____

## Prayer Requests

_____
_____
_____
_____
_____

## CHAPTER 10

# Worry Free?

*"And God will exalt you in due time, if you humble yourselves under his mighty hand by casting all your cares on him because he cares for you."*

1 PETER 5:6-7

> *Yet we all ask, "What if...?" It's an unfinished question punctuated by the ellipses of fear, and it is ultimately rooted in a lack of trust in God. The big picture of anxiety always stems from this source. Fear exposes where we do not fully trust God. (Exchanging Mirrors, pg. 168).*

Life provides ample opportunities for fear, yet followers in the Lord Jesus have the resources to live life free from anxiety. Yet are we willing to practice these commands outlined in 1 Peter to experience a worry-free life?

**READ:** 1 Peter 5, Matthew 6:25-27, *Exchanging Mirrors* pgs. 167-179.

1. Given the circumstances of Peter's original audience, why might these verses have been particularly encouraging? Why might this command have been difficult?

2. How does the Gospel help us answer the "big questions" of is God good? Is He powerful? Is He sovereign?

3. In what way has God provided "something better" (Hebrews 11:40) for us? How is this an encouragement as we face unexplainable trials?

4. God's sovereignty is a recurring theme in 1 Peter. Think about God's foreknowledge described in 1 Peter 1:2 and the exultation He has promised in "due time" (1 Peter 5:6). How does God's supremacy over time and world events offer hope in suffering?

5. Do your thought patterns communicate a spirit that trusts the heart of God?

6. The author outlines what she calls, the "anxiety continuum"- a relentless cycle of anxiety, false hope, and discouragement. What alternative is offered in 1 Peter 5:6-7? How does applying these principles grant freedom from anxiety?

# Notes

_____

_____

_____

_____

_____


# Prayer Requests

_____

_____

_____

_____

_____

# CHAPTER 11
## In the End

*"And, after you have suffered a little while, the God of all grace who has called you to his eternal glory in Christ will himself restore, confirm, strengthen, and establish you. To him belongs the power forever. Amen."*

1 PETER 5:10-11

*In the end we know that God has promised us great and glorious truths, for He is the all-powerful One. But we cannot know or understand how great He is or His promises are until they are before us in greater glory and splendor than our minds can imagine. (Exchanging Mirrors, pg. 190).*

Through faith in the Lord Jesus, we are given opportunity to live and die well. We are granted the strength to have confidence in the worst of life circumstances, knowing our sure hope in Christ.

**READ:** 1 Peter. Look for reasons that Peter gives for hope to the persecuted church. What reasons for hope can you personalize from this epistle? *Exchanging Mirrors* pgs. 181-191.

1. Peter addresses the reality of suffering in the closing words of this epistle. What hope does he offer to the believers as the "after" to their suffering?

2. In a few words, how should a believer be described in the face of suffering?

3. What were some of the directives Peter gave for suffering rightly? (See page 182).

4. In this chapter, the author explores a few facets of the Lord's character. What attribute of God can you worship Him for today? Find a Scripture passage that describes that aspect of God's character.

5. In contrasting the mirror of empowerment with the mirror of the Gospel, the author writes;

> "The gospel gives us faith in the midst of crushing circumstances, love in the face of hate, strength in the face of fear, and confidence in the face of death. Aren't these the things that everyone longs for?" (Exchanging Mirrors, pg. 187).

Read Romans 8:35-39. What is the Christ-follower's true hope?

6. How have you been challenged to more fully understand or reconsider your Gospel-given identity through this study?

# Notes

_____
_____
_____
_____
_____

# Prayer Requests

_____
_____
_____
_____
_____

# Answered Prayers!

## About the Author

**KATHERINE HAGER** is passionate about encouraging women through Biblically-saturated written content. In 2019, she launched EquippedMama—an online ministry to encourage Christian mothers through Scripture-based books and blogs. She released *Redeeming Mama; Purpose-Filled Prayers for Your Newborn* in 2019 and the Spanish translation in the summer of 2020. Katherine lives in central Texas with her husband and three children. When she is not writing, she enjoys being in the year-round sunshine with her family and visiting with friends over things of the Lord.

**ALSO CHECK OUT** Katherine's other book—*Redeeming Mama: Purpose-Filled Prayers for Your Newborn*. Available in both English and Spanish at Amazon.com.

## PRAYER WILL CHANGE YOUR BABY'S LIFE.

For many mothers, the job description of raising a little one, or several children, can seem daunting. Besides the never- ending to-do list, physical and emotional demands, and the eternal lack of time, there is the constant struggle of wondering—does what I do matter? Is there anything I can do to contribute to the eternal welfare of my child?

There is.

In *Redeeming Mama*, Katherine Hager meets mamas from all places in life and encourages them to walk through the Psalms and commit to a lifestyle of prayer. Through this six-week prayer journey, she models how mothers might start their prayer ministry to their families, and inspires them to use each moment to establish a spiritual legacy for their children.

*Write Katherine a review on* **amazon**

Made in the USA
Coppell, TX
11 February 2026

71745643R00031